Action Sports Library

Scuba Diving

Bob Italia

Published by Abdo & Daughters, 4940 Viking Drive, Suite 622, Edina, Minnesota 55435.

Library bound edition distributed by Rockbottom Books, Pentagon Tower, P.O. Box 36036, Minneapolis, Minnesota 55435.

Printed in the United States.

Cover Photo credit: Peter Arnold, Inc.
Interior Photo credits: Alfred K. Peterson/Firth Photobank—p. 23, 31
Peter Arnold, Inc.—p. 4, 12, 15, 27
Frozen Images—p. 7, 9, 15, 25, 28

Edited By Kal Gronvall

Warning: The series *Action Sports Library* is intended as entertainment for children. These sporting activities should never be attempted without proper conditioning, training, instruction, supervision, and equipment.

Library of Congress Cataloging-in-Publication Data

Italia, Bob, 1955-
    Scuba diving / Bob Italia
    p. cm. -- (Action sports library)
    ISBN 1-56239-345-6
    1. Scuba diving--Juvenile literature. I. Title II. Series:
    Italia, Bob, 1955- Action sports library.
    GV840.S78I84 1994
    797.2'3--dc20   94-3590
                                          CIP
                                          AC

Contents

Scuba diving is
fascinating, exciting. . .and
a little bit scary.

Breathing Underwater

The first time a person goes underwater with scuba gear is always a thrilling experience. All of the incredible sensations that the new diver experiences when he or she first takes the tank and regulator under the surface are based on one thing: The fact that suddenly they can relax on the bottom and breathe.

Being able to stay underwater and not have to hold your breath is a sensation that no instructor can prepare a student for with words. Not until the water closes over your head and all sound disappears except for the roar of your own breathing can you know what it is like. It is fascinating, exciting, and a bit scary. It takes several breaths before you are willing to trust this amazing feat.

An Ancient Activity

The sport of scuba diving is fairly new. But people were diving at least as early as 1000 B.C. Ancient historians mention that rulers often used divers in their local battles. Xerxes of Persia around 475 B.C. used divers to recover treasure. Even Alexander the Great was lowered in a barrel to look at the diver's world. One of Alexander's victories at Tyree, around 330 B.C., was aided by underwater swimmers.

Throughout history, underwater swimmers and divers have been used by the military of countries that waged battles on water. Today we have the Navy SEAL Team which is very active in underwater warfare.

The first scuba operation took place in 1825, when a man named James constructed a belt that would carry air. The diver breathed the air from the belt. But the belt could not carry enough air to last more than a few minutes.

By 1880, Englishman Henry Fleuss developed a scuba device that used pure oxygen. The rig worked well but the diver had to be very careful. Oxygen under certain pressure conditions becomes a deadly gas to humans.

Fleuss's device was improved and used by the U.S. Navy in World War II. It was a long-lasting closed unit which would not let off bubbles to give away the presence of a diver.

The real diving breakthrough took place when a steel tank was developed that held compressed air. This allowed the diver to stay underwater a long time.

The first use of the steel tank was with a full-face mask. The air flowed through the mask and the diver breathed it. It worked well but much air was wasted, thus cutting down diving time.

In the early 1940s, Frenchman Jacques-Yves Cousteau developed an underwater regulator. This regulator conserved air by releasing only the amount of air the diver needed to breathe. It increased underwater diving time to one hour.

The Cousteau unit was also simple and inexpensive. Even more, it marked the beginning of the sport of scuba diving. ("SCUBA" stands for "Self-Contained Underwater Breathing Apparatus.") The sport grew slowly through the late '40s and early '50s because of one reason: In most parts of the world divers became so chilled they were forced to leave the water after a short stay.

It was in the early 1950s that rubber suits were designed and made available to the public. The first ones used were made of a thin sheet of rubber that covered the body like a rubber glove covers the hand. They kept the diver warm.

These old "dry suits" were worn over long underwear and sweat suits or sweaters. The clothing acted as an insulator and the rubber suit simply kept the insulation dry. However, the dry suits were so thin they were easily punctured. As soon as a leak developed, the clothing underneath became wet and all insulation properties were lost.

World-renowned explorer Jacques-Yves Cousteau invented the regulator which gave birth to scuba diving.

With the advent of the "dry suit" to keep the diver warm, the number enjoying the sport took a jump. But it wasn't until a new device called the "wet suit" was introduced that things really began to happen. The wet suit actually trapped a thin layer of water next to the diver's body. The water soon heated up to body temperature and acted as additional insulation.

One of the early wet suits was made by Terry Cox in a little shop located in Newport Beach, California. Mr. Cox experimented with several materials, one of which was foam polyvinyl chloride. This suit was warm but would not stand up under use. Finally, neoprene foam was selected as the best material available. When the wet suit hit the market, the average person could go diving in relative comfort.

As the market grew larger, ready-made suits appeared in extra small, small, medium, medium large, large, and extra large sizes. Today, almost anyone can walk into a store and walk out with a well-fitted wet suit.

Diving Equipment

Diving equipment is extensive and varied. Basic diving equipment around the world includes a mask, fins, and a snorkel.

The Mask

The diver's mask performs several important functions. First, it traps air in front of the eyes so the light passes through the air before it enters the eye. Secondly, it also helps to keep water from running up your nose and getting into your sinuses. Finally, it allows you to blow air out your nose to relieve the extra pressure that builds as you descend.

The most important thing to consider when buying a mask is whether it fits your face and makes a comfortable seal to keep out the water. A simple test to check for a proper fit is to place the mask on your face without the straps being in place. Now inhale slightly through the nose. This will create a vacuum in the mask. Now let go of it. It should stay in place if it fits properly.

Some masks have a purge valve, a one-way valve located in the bottom of the mask. It allows the diver to remove water from the mask by exhaling through his nose. In most cases, however, it is faster and easier to remove air from a mask without a purge valve.

Masks and the Glasses-Wearer

If you wear glasses and can't see well enough to be comfortable without them, you should wear corrective lenses when you dive. If you wear contacts, you can still wear them while you dive. In this case, a mask with a purge will help you to avoid losing contacts if they are accidentally washed out.

The safest way to see properly underwater is to have your prescription placed in your faceplate glass.

The mask should make a comfortable seal to keep water out.

The Fins

Fins allow the diver to imitate the way underwater mammals swim.

There are two major types of fins. One type is similar to a shoe. Your foot slips into a rubber shoe with a fin blade attached to it. The other type has a pocket for your foot and is strapped behind the heel to hold your foot in the pocket.

Fins must be comfortable. Fins that are too tight will cause cramps and cold feet due to loss of circulation. Fins that are too loose will slip back and forth on your feet and rub sores.

Heel strap fins are generally more comfortable if you wear rubber booties. The booties serve several functions. They keep the fins from rubbing your feet raw, they keep your feet warm, and they help you walk on the beach and over the rocks. If you decide to buy heel strap fins, ones that have a replaceable strap are best.

Fin sizes run small, medium, large, and extra large. The size of the fins should match the size and strength of the diver. Smaller fins generally work well for most beginning divers. The more you swim, the larger the fins you can use.

Snorkeling

A snorkel is a breathing tube extending above the water. It is used to swim just below the surface.

The snorkel enables you to see better because it allows you to keep your face down in the water, letting your eyes adjust to the reduced light.

Snorkels come in all sizes and shapes. You want one that will give you all the air you need with as little restriction as possible. The smaller the tube, the more restriction there is. So you want a fairly large tube. Get a tube large enough so that your thumb will fit into the end of it.

Your snorkel should also be comfortable in your mouth. It should not push or pull on your lips. It should fit very easily in place and you shouldn't have to bite on it to hold it there.

Some advanced snorkels have a plastic mouth piece that the diver first dips in hot water to soften it. Then the diver places it in the mouth and bites down on it. The mouth piece forms right to the diver's mouth, giving a very comfortable custom fit.

SECONDARY EQUIPMENT

Secondary equipment is not needed for all divers under all conditions. But each piece is absolutely necessary under certain conditions or types of diving.

The Buoyancy Compensator

The buoyancy compensator (BC) or a flotation vest is a must for all scuba and snorkel diving if you don't use a wet suit and a weight belt. In breath-hold diving, the BC is a safety device designed to float the diver on the surface. If the diver is wearing a wet suit and a weight belt, there is no need for the BC. If trouble occurs, the diver can drop the weight belt and float to the surface.

When the diver is not wearing a wet suit, a BC should be worn. If the diver has trouble, such as cramps, the BC acts as a surface flotation device.

For scuba divers, the BC becomes much more than a safety device. The BC has high amounts of buoyancy and can lift a diver's chest high out of the water.

There are two basic types of BCs. One is like a jacket that inflates. The other is like a donut on your back—generally called a back inflation unit (BIU). The jacket type does a much better job of acting as a safety device because it floats the diver straight up on the surface.

The wet suit acts as an insulator against cold water.

All BCs have certain things in common. They can hold as much as the diver needs. The diver can add air from the tank by pressing a button, or by blowing air into it from a manual inflator.

It is very important that new divers practice both methods until they learn when to add air and how much. All units have a manual deflation valve, and an automatic over-inflation valve. The diver must learn to use the manual deflation valve properly. The diver should learn not to inflate the unit to the point where the automatic over-inflation valve activates. Doing so will cause the diver to rise to the surface too fast, creating all kinds of physical problems.

The Wet Suit

The wet suit is a tight-fitting coverall made of neoprene, which is composed, in part, of bubbles. The gas in the bubbles conducts heat more slowly than water, so the suit acts as an insulator against cold water. The thicker the wet suit, the longer the diver stays warm.

The thinner the suit, however, the more comfortable it is and the less tired the diver will become swimming in it. The thickness of the suit a diver will want depends on the temperature of the water, the diver's size and physiology, and the length of time the diver spends in the water.

Getting in and out of any wet suit can be difficult. Experienced divers put a small amount of liquid dishwashing soap in a plastic bottle and fill the bottle with water. If the dive site has hot water, fill the bottle with hot water. Splash some soapy water in the suit and slide in.

The Weight Belt

The weight belt is used to counteract buoyancy. All weight belts have one thing in common: they can be quickly unfastened with one hand, and dropped if an emergency arises.

There are two types of standard release buckles. The best is the webbed belt. It is pulled through the buckle until tight. Then the buckle is pressed down to lock it. It is easy to add or subtract weight on the webbed belt. And it can be tightened easily while diving.

The wire hookover type also works well. But is very time-consuming and difficult to adjust. Some of the newer belts are made of neoprene rubber instead of webbing.

The Regulator

Regulators are simple but require special tools and gauges for proper setting. All regulators work on what is called the "demand system." This means you must inhale through your mouthpiece before the air comes out. All tanks have two regulators, the primary and the secondary. The primary regulator is the main regulator and the secondary regulator is used as an alternate air source.

Both primary and secondary regulators operate the same way. The principle behind all regulators is to break down the high pressure air from the tank to a lower pressure, which the diver can breathe, generally around 140 pounds per square inch (p.s.i.).

Underwater Pressure Gauges

The underwater pressure gauge is attached to your regulator or to your tank. This gauge indicates how much air you have left in your tank(s) at any given time. This pressure gauge should be on your regulator, not on the tank. It will receive less of a beating if stored with the regulator than if stored with the tank.

Tanks

Tanks come in several sizes: 80 cubic feet, 71.2 cubic feet, 60 cubic feet, and 50 cubic feet. All tanks can be put into a double harness and rigged together so that you end up with double 80's or double 71.2's, etc. Every tank must be stamped by the U.S.

Regulators break down the high pressure air in the tank to a lower, more breathable pressure.

Department of Transportation, indicating its working pressure. If you buy a regular scuba tank from a shop, all the controls are in force. All you have to do is pick the size you want.

Tank Valves

There are only two types of tank valves in use today, the "J" valve and the "K" valve. The difference in function of the "J" valve and the "K" valve is significant. The "K" valve is simply an on-off valve. (An underwater pressure gauge is a must if a "K" valve is used.)

The "J" valve is also an on-off valve with one additional feature. It has a spring-loaded lever mechanism which releases about 300 to 400 pounds of reserve air pressure from the tank in case of an emergency. If you suddenly realize it has become difficult to breathe, all you have to do is pull the lever and you have enough reserve air supply to reach the surface safely. The ideal set-up is to have a "J" valve with an underwater pressure gauge.

Every air tank must have a U.S. Department of Transportation approval stamp.

Backpacks

Most divers prefer to wear some kind of a backpack or tank harness. Most backpacks are built into the BC units. Both the back inflation units and the various BC jackets are designed to act also as a backpack for your tank.

The Diver's Float

Some divers take a float with them to the diving area.

Two of the most common inexpensive floats are the inner tube and the surf mat. Either one can be used as a rescue device.

Divers usually attach hooks to the floats so they can hang their flag, cameras, lights, goodie bags or anything else they might need on the dive. Sometimes a long swim is needed to get to a good diving spot. In such cases, many divers use special "boards" or kayak-type boats as a combination float and transportation. Be sure to choose a float that fits your needs.

The Diver Console

Most of the gauges the diver needs are worn on a diver console. The console is located on the end of a hose coming from the first stage of the regulator. All consoles have a tank pressure gauge and a depth gauge. Some consoles have a compass and a diving timer.

The Depth Gauge

The depth gauge is very important to the scuba diver. There are two types of depth gauges on the market, the oil-filled gauge and the air-filled gauge. The oil-filled gauge is more expensive but it lasts much longer than the air-filled gauge.

The Diver's Watch

Every diver should keep time on his dive. (If he or she is diving deeper than 30 feet, keeping time is very important in avoiding the possibility of the bends.) Watches can be used to coordinate your dive with others. Two buddy pairs could finish their dives at the same time in the same area so they can swim back to the boat in a group. Watches can also be used for navigation purposes.

Dive Timers

The dive timer is a stop watch that turns itself on and turns itself off without the diver having to think about it. The dive timer turns itself on at about 6-8 feet as the diver starts to dive and the pressure increases. It turns off at 6-8 feet as the diver comes back to the surface, giving the diver an accurate time for the dive. Keeping an accurate time for each dive is very important when making multiple or repetitive dives.

Diving Computers

Diving computers replace the console and perform the functions of the underwater pressure gauge, the depth gauge, and a timing device. They monitor the information from these three gauges. They compute such things as time left on this dive with the air left in your tank, any decompression needed, what your maximum depth was, and your surface interval.

DEVELOPING DIVING SKILLS

Basic swimming skills are required of a beginning diver. You must also understand the specific function of each item of equipment and know how to use it in the proper manner. You will also be expected to know how to use each piece of diving equipment to successfully pass a scuba course.

Using the Mask

The first thing to master is putting the mask on. Place the mask on your face and pull the strap over your head. Do not put the strap over the back of your head and pull the mask down over your face.

Put the mask on first, then pull the strap over your head. This can be easily done with one hand by sucking in just a little with the nose to create a vacuum. This will hold the mask in place while you place the strap over your head.

The strap should be positioned carefully around the back of the head. If it is too high or too low, the pressure around the mask against the face will not be even and the mask may leak. If the strap is too tight, it will give you a headache. If the strap is too loose the mask will leak. Take time and do it right. Proper strap position is very important.

Once your mask is on, swim with it for awhile and get used to it. You will notice that things look bigger. The magnification is due to a physical law of light called refraction. Pick things up and get used to the magnification, so you won't be frightened by a passing fish.

Mask flooding happens quite often. Depending upon the type of mask you have, purge or non-purge, the technique to clear the mask of water is slightly different.

If the mask is a purge mask, then the purge valve should be the lowest point. Clearing the mask is accomplished by looking at a 45° angle towards the bottom, holding the entire mask firmly in place, and exhaling through the nose. When using the non-purge mask, the diver wants to make the lowest edge of the mask where it seals against the upper lip the lowest point, so the water will run out and leave the mask clear. Clearing the mask is accomplished by looking at a 45° angle towards the surface of the water, holding the top and sides of the mask (but not the bottom) firmly in place, and exhaling through the nose. When done properly, no air should escape except a small bubble which indicates that all the water is gone from the mask. A good diver can clear his mask four or five times on one breath.

If your mask fogs up on you so you can't see clearly, there are two things you can do. First, before you dive, wash it (toothpaste is good) to make sure that there is no grease of any kind on it. Then spit into it before each dive. Do this before you wet it in the water. Rub the saliva around the inside of the glass as well as around the outside. Then rinse the mask off and wear it. It should stay clear.

Using the Fins

To get the maximum effectiveness from the fins, the diver's toes must be pointed, and the legs slightly bent at the knees. This places the fins in a position to push the water backwards on both the upward stroke and downward stroke. If the fins are not in this position, they will move up and down in the water but will not push the diver forward.

Another common error is called bicycling. Bicycling occurs when the diver brings his knees toward his stomach, much like the leg action of riding a bicycle. The fins move a great distance in the water but the motion is back and forth and produces little or no thrust.

Using the Snorkel

The position of the snorkel on the mask is important. The snorkel should be on the left side. Later, when the diver learns to use scuba gear, the air supply from the scuba will come over the right shoulder. If the snorkel is always on the left and scuba always on the right, even in a stress situation there is no chance of a mix-up.

The snorkel should be held on by a snorkel-keeper that comes with every snorkel. Both holes in the keeper go over the snorkel. The strap goes between the snorkel and the narrow part of the keeper to hold the snorkel firmly in place on the outside of the strap, not between the mask strap and the head. With the mask in place on the face, the snorkel should be adjusted by sliding it back and forth on the strap. It should also be adjusted up and down in the keeper until it fits in the mouth naturally without having to be held there with tight jaws. This adjustment is critical for proper use and comfort.

BECOMING A CERTIFIED SCUBA DIVER

After the diver has learned how to use the mask, fins, and snorkel, he or she is ready to learn scuba diving. But you must become certified as a diver before you can take the plunge. To become a certified diver, students must attend diving instruction classes taught by qualified scuba instructors.

In the United States, there are several national organizations which qualify their scuba instructors. Ask to see your instructor's certification card. (A nationally recognized certification card is a must.) Discuss with the instructor the type of training they have had and the number of hours involved in their training before you pick an instructor. If their training consisted of only one or two weekends, it is not enough. They must have attended at least five or six weekend sessions to be properly trained as an instructor. Choose your instructor carefully. It can be a life-or-death decision.

Skills to be Performed for Scuba Diver Certification

(A) From a scuba unit placed on the bottom in four feet of water, be able to:

1. Swim down, pick up the regulator, and breathe from it.
2. Clear the mask while breathing from the unit.
3. Fill a flotation vest with the oral inflator, while breathing from the unit underwater.
4. Swim from one scuba unit to another scuba unit without surfacing.
5. Swim down and breathe from a single regulator with another person, alternating every two breaths, for 2 or 3 minutes.

(B) In a pool with a tank on your back, be able to perform a series of underwater maneuvers.

THE BUDDY SYSTEM

Divers should always use the buddy system. In this system, your buddy checks your gear and you check your buddy's gear just before you enter the water. Then the two buddies stay close enough together that if one needs to be helped in any way, the buddy is right there to help.

Being able to help a fellow diver is most important. As a buddy, part of your responsibility is to recognize when your partner needs help. To do this you must be actively aware of your buddy and what they are doing. This awareness should start on the beach or in the boat, *before* you enter the water. A general discussion of what the two of you plan to do is important. This "pre-dive plan" may take the form of a five-minute chat while you are getting suited up.

Any special signals can be worked out and old signals reviewed to insure they mean the same thing to both of you. Particularly important are the signals for "I'm out of air," "I'm going up," "I need to buddy-breathe," and "I need help." These signals vary from area to area and should be clear in both divers' minds *before* the dive.

The next important aid the buddies should give each other is an inspection of each other's gear after they are suited up. Make sure the weight belt is clear in case it needs to be dropped. Make sure the flap on the wet suit jacket or snap on the wet suit crotch is snapped.   And check to be certain everything looks in order for the dive.

When entering the water, the main concern with your buddy is that he or she is comfortable and not under stress. There are signs that will aid you in knowing how relaxed your buddy is. Watch his or her breathing. If it is short and rapid, then your buddy is not relaxed. Slow down the pace and come up for a chat.

One of the best ways to determine how your buddy really feels is to watch his or her feet. If he or she is kicking in a relaxed slow kick, then he or she is okay. But if his or her feet are really working, trouble is at hand. Take some weights off your buddy, inflate the BC or do whatever else seems to ease his or her mind so he or she can relax.

What if you miss your buddy's warning or distress signs and your buddy panics? You must drop your buddy's weight belt. Put your regulator in your mouth and come up behind your buddy underwater. Watch out for your buddy's feet and tank. Reach around and undo your buddy's belt and make sure it drops off. Panic victims will often arch their back to keep their head up. This will pinch the belt under the tank. Don't let your buddy take hold of your tank. If you can inflate your buddy's vest, do so. Do not take off your buddy's mask. It will keep water out of his or her eyes and nose, which will help calm him or her down. Then swim back to the beach or boat. Do not pull a diver by the collar of his or her flotation vest. This will tend to choke him or her. You can tow your buddy by the tank, pulling your fellow diver back if he or she needs help.

What do you do if your buddy gets a bad leg cramp? Leg cramps can be very painful, especially if the cramp is in the thigh area. Most cramps fortunately are in the calf. Although they hurt and hinder swimming a great deal, they do not tend to panic the diver. The best thing to do is to stretch the muscle out as soon as possible. This means stretching the leg out and bringing the toe back as far as possible towards the head. Rubbing or kneading the cramped area helps too.

If the cramp will not go away there is a good swimming assist you can do to help your buddy back to dry ground where he can work out the cramp. This swimming assist is good also if your buddy just gets tired and needs a "push."

In case of emergencies, divers should always use the buddy system when diving.

ENTERING THE WATER

Whether you are diving into a pool or into the ocean, there are two types of entries into the water: the front entry and the back entry. A few basics remain the same in each case:

1. Hold the mask in place with your hand. Place the right hand with the palm directly over the nose, the fingers spread out over the top of the mask and the thumb under the lower edge. The hand then holds the mask in place and covers the glass in case the diver slips and falls into the water in a face-flop position. Doing this could break the glass in his or her face.

2. Check the water carefully before you jump in. Make sure it is deep enough so that you won't hit bottom.

3. Have all of your gear in place and checked out before you make the entry.

4. If you want to stay shallow when you jump in, spread out your arms and legs as you hit. You'll stop right on the surface. If you are going in from an awkward place such as from a small boat, just roll over the side in a little ball.

On any entry, the important things are to hold everything in place, to make sure the entry area is safe, and to hit the water in such a way that you do not hurt yourself.

The ocean entry situations most commonly encountered are sand and rock entries. On a sand entry, the diver just walks out, puts his fins on, and enters. If it is a no-surf entry, he walks out until he is waist deep, puts his fins on and swims out. If there is surf he puts his fins on, enters the water in a backward shuffle, then swims out.

Surf Entries

Surf entries are easy if you remember a few rules:

1. Never stand up in the surf.
2. Get through the surf line as fast as you can. Don't stop to adjust something halfway through.
3. Never let a breaker catch you broadside. Be either head into it or feet into it so you will not be rolled sideways.
4. Hold your mask on with your hand every time a breaker goes over you. It will come off if you don't.
5. Always go *under* a wave, never over it. Remember, the force of a breaker is *on top*. If you dive under the white water, the force is far less.
6. Once you start out or in, don't stop until you are clear of the surf.

A diver should not tackle surf that is too heavy. Never go diving through the surf if you are frightened. Unless you are confident of your ability to handle it, you can panic very quickly if you should

A diver needs to hold the mask when entering the water.

lose a fin, mask, or get tumbled. The surf is a dangerous environment and must be treated as such.

Surf entries are variable because surf conditions are so variable. There are three basic ways to enter the surf:

1. All gear on and in place. The diver walks backwards into the surf with fins on. The diver keeps a close watch on the surf by looking behind so a wave does not sneak up and knock the diver down. This is a good entry when the beach is steep and the break zone (area of white water) small.

2. All gear on and in place. The diver gets on hands and knees and crawls into the water. As soon as the water is a foot or so deep, the diver starts to swim with his or her fins and "dog paddles" with his or her hands. This type of entry is sometimes called a "polliwog." It is a good entry if the bottom is rocky and irregular.

3. All gear on and in place except for the fins which are held in the hand. The diver walks in frontwards until he or she gets waist or chest deep, then puts on his or her fins and swims out. This is a good entry if the slope of the beach is slight and there is a long surf line. The diver must remember to use a "shuffle" type step as he or she goes out so as not to step on a stingray.

WRECK DIVING

The waters of the world have shipwrecks of many kinds in them. A wreck is always a fascinating place to dive. But it could become dangerous if the diver is not careful. You should not approach a wreck from the current side. Many wrecks have spikes and extrusions sticking out from them which the current could push you against, causing you severe injury. Always approach a wreck from the down-current side.

Make sure you understand a wreck from the outside before you go in. Looking at the outside of a wreck is an adventure in itself and not all that dangerous. Once you go inside, however, you get into an area that can rapidly become dangerous. If the wreck is a large one, you must realize that you are entering a giant maze. In many cases, you cannot always see well enough to get out of a wreck once you are in it. So be careful.

In wreck diving you need a lifeline and lights. At times, you can enter a wreck and see quite well. But as you swim along, the fine sediments that have settled·inside are stirred up behind you in the water by your fins. As a result, when you turn around to come out you can't see anything. A lifeline is an absolute must!

Even if you have all the necessary things like lifelines, and a tender to watch the line, plus bright lights, you should still not go too far into this maze of wood and steel. You should never be in the wreck so far that you cannot hold your breath and swim to the outside to make an emergency ascent. Again, a flotation vest is a consideration. If you are deep in a wreck, you should not wear it. It may trap you.

Wrecks offer divers fascinating places to explore.

Divers should understand a wreck from the outside before they go in. The inside of a wreck can become a dangerous maze.

Plan all wreck dives carefully and follow your dive plan. It is mandatory that everyone know what to expect so there will be as little confusion as possible.

Collecting souvenirs in wrecks is a no-no. A wreck should not be disturbed so the next diver can enjoy it, too.

NIGHT DIVING

Night diving is very similar to day diving except that buddies must stay very close together so as not to lose each other. If you are in the ocean at night, turn off your light and let your eyes become accustomed to the darkness. You will see all kinds of little things moving in the water. The barnacles on the rocks will appear to be little flashing stars in the sky. Such sights can add up to some of the most memorable diving experiences you have ever had.

A practical rule for all night diving is to always dive in the area first in the daytime so that you are totally familiar with it. Only then, venture out to investigate it at night. Following are some general diving safety rules everyone should observe.

DIVING SAFETY RULES

1. Make sure you are in good physical and mental condition; dive only when feeling well.
2. Maintain good swimming ability.
3. Take a certified diving class from a nationally recognized organization.
4. Get skin diving experience; this is a prerequisite to scuba diving.
5. Take first-aid training.
6. Be current in lifesaving techniques.
7. Have a first-aid kit.
8. Know your limitations (both personal and equipment).
9. Check and use proper equipment in good condition.
10. Use a buoyancy compensator.

11. Attach your weight belt with a quick release so that it can be detached with one hand.
12. Plan your dive.
13. Know your diving area.
14. Limit depth to less than 60 feet.
15. Dive with a buddy and stay together.
16. Develop and use methods of underwater communication.
17. Treat spear guns as dangerous weapons.
18. Equalize pressure before pain is felt.
19. Leave water when injured, tired, or cold.
20. Surface carefully and correctly.
21. Breathe regularly with scuba.
22. Avoid stage decompression or decompression repetitive dives.
23. Use only pure compressed air.
24. Maintain and handle compressed air cylinders properly.
25. In general: Know what you are doing; use good judgment and common sense; be prepared for emergencies; avoid panic; practice diving skills; read and study about diving and related activities, use moderation in depth and time in water; build up experience gradually under safe conditions; before diving do not indulge in alcohol, overeat, or eat gas producing foods.

To enjoy scuba diving, all divers should know what they are doing, and use good judgement and common sense.

Glossary

atmosphere—the surrounding influence.

BIU—back inflation unit.

buoyancy—the ability to float or rise when submerged in water.

console—a panel on which dials, gauges, etc. are mounted.

decompression—to release from pressure.

dry suit—a close-fitting waterproof rubber suit.

float—something that floats on the water surface.

gauge—an instrument for measuring.

insulation—something that prevents the passage of heat.

neoprene—a man-made rubber that is oil resistant.

purge—to remove what is harmful.

regulator—a device that controls the amount of air intake.

scuba—self-contained underwater breathing apparatus.

snorkel—a curved tube which enables swimmers to breathe underwater while swimming near the surface.

wet suit—a close-fitting suit made of material that traps a thin layer of water against the body to retain body heat.